HAL•LEONARD
INSTRUMENTAL
PLAY-ALONG

AUDIO ACCESS
INCLUDED

Songs from
**Frozen, Tangled
and Enchanted**

CONTENTS

To access audio visit:
www.halleonard.com/mylibrary

Enter Code
4481-3647-0357-3139

Audio Arrangements by Peter Deneff

ISBN 978-1-4803-8730-0

WALT DISNEY MUSIC COMPANY
WONDERLAND MUSIC COMPANY, INC.

DISTRIBUTED BY

HAL•LEONARD®
CORPORATION
7777 W. BLUEMOUND RD. P.O. BOX 13819 MILWAUKEE, WI 53213

In Australia Contact:
Hal Leonard Australia Pty. Ltd.
4 Lentara Court
Cheltenham, Victoria, 3192 Australia
Email: ausadmin@halleonard.com.au

Visit Hal Leonard Online at
www.halleonard.com

DO YOU WANT TO BUILD A SNOWMAN?

from Disney's Animated Feature FROZEN

CELLO

Music and Lyrics by KRISTEN ANDERSON-LOPEZ
and ROBERT LOPEZ

FOR THE FIRST TIME IN FOREVER

from Disney's Animated Feature FROZEN

CELLO

Music and Lyrics by KRISTEN ANDERSON-LOPEZ
and ROBERT LOPEZ

HAPPY WORKING SONG

from Walt Disneys Pictures' ENCHANTED

Music by ALAN MENKEN
Lyrics by STEPHEN SCHWARTZ

CELLO

Moderately
Strings

I SEE THE LIGHT

from Walt Disney Pictures' TANGLED

CELLO

Music by ALAN MENKEN
Lyrics by GLENN SLATER

poco rit.   a tempo

rit.   **mp**

I'VE GOT A DREAM

from Walt Disney Pictures' TANGLED

CELLO

Music by ALAN MENKEN
Lyrics by GLENN SLATER

IN SUMMER
from Disney's Animated Feature FROZEN

CELLO

Music and Lyrics by KRISTEN ANDERSON-LOPEZ
and ROBERT LOPEZ

LET IT GO
from Disney's Animated Feature FROZEN

CELLO

Music and Lyrics by KRISTEN ANDERSON-LOPEZ
and ROBERT LOPEZ

LOVE IS AN OPEN DOOR

from Disney's Animated Feature FROZEN

CELLO

Music and Lyrics by KRISTEN ANDERSON-LOPEZ
and ROBERT LOPEZ

MOTHER KNOWS BEST
from Walt Disney Pictures' TANGLED

CELLO

Music by ALAN MENKEN
Lyrics by GLENN SLATER

SO CLOSE
from Walt Disney Pictures' ENCHANTED

Music by ALAN MENKEN
Lyrics by STEPHEN SCHWARTZ

CELLO

THAT'S HOW YOU KNOW
from Walt Disney Pictures' ENCHANTED

CELLO

Music by ALAN MENKEN
Lyrics by STEPHEN SCHWARTZ

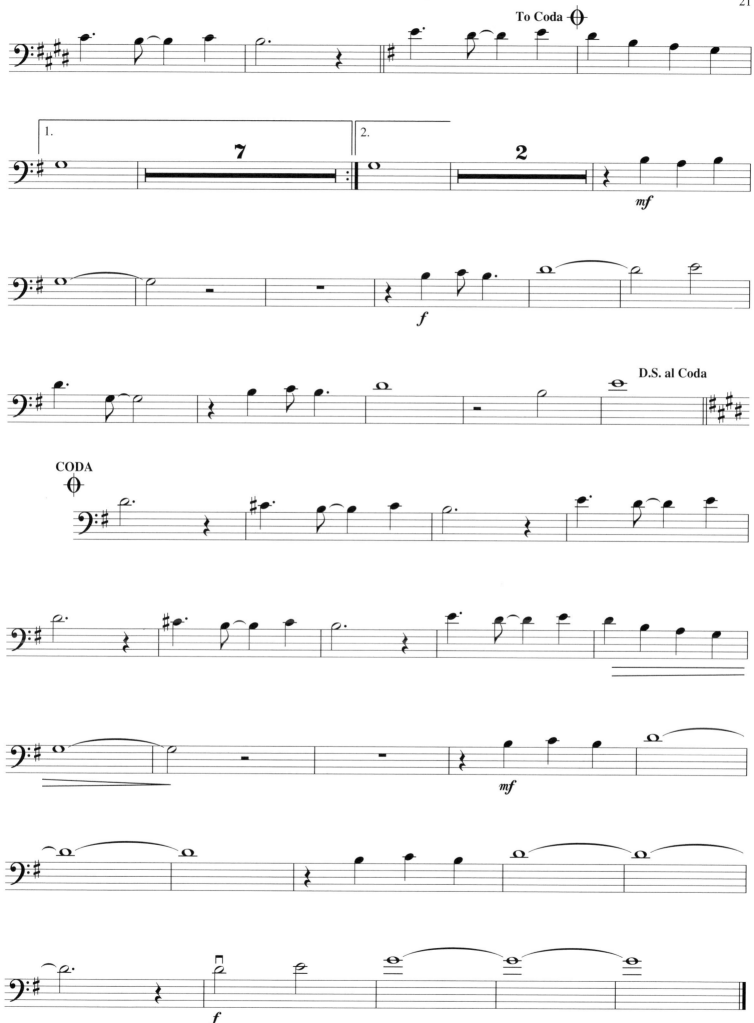

TRUE LOVE'S KISS

from Walt Disney Pictures' ENCHANTED

CELLO

Music by ALAN MENKEN
Lyrics by STEPHEN SCHWARTZ

WHEN WILL MY LIFE BEGIN

from Walt Disney Pictures' TANGLED

Music by ALAN MENKEN
Lyrics by GLENN SLATER

CELLO